I Feel Sleepy

By Cameron Macintosh

Let's sleep!

I sleep up in a tree.

It's a den!

A den is a little gap
in a tree.

I feel very snug!

I sleep up here!

I sleep in a nest
on this big sill.

I can see lots of things
from here.

I do not get dizzy,
so I will not drop off the sill!

I sleep in a rocky den.

When it's cold,
I have a deep sleep
for weeks and weeks!

I get very fluffy
so I can keep snug.

I come out when
I am hungry!

I dig and dig to sleep
down deep.

No one can creep up on me when I sleep!

I feel happy in this bed.

I sleep in a gap in this tree.

It could seem odd,
but I sleep in the day!

The cold can not get to me.

I am still a baby.

I sleep in Mum's sack!

I feel happy in here,
and I sleep well.

I am very snug in Mum's sack,
but I can peep out if I want!

CHECKING FOR MEANING

1. How does the squirrel feel when it sleeps in its den? *(Literal)*

2. Which creature sleeps during the day? *(Literal)*

3. Why does the bear become very hungry in the rocky den? *(Inferential)*

EXTENDING VOCABULARY

deep	What is a *deep* sleep? Do you ever have a deep sleep? How do you sleep if you have a deep sleep? What other things can be described as deep? E.g. water.
creep	What does it mean to *creep*? Is this a quiet movement or a loud movement? What are other words with a similar meaning? E.g. tiptoe, sneak.
sack	What is a *sack*? What is another word with a similar meaning? E.g. bag, pouch. Why is the baby koala *snug* in the sack?

MOVING BEYOND THE TEXT

1. How would you describe your bedroom?

2. Are all children's bedrooms the same? How are they similar and different?

3. Why do animals choose particular places to sleep?

4. Imagine you are another animal and explain where you would sleep and why.

SPELLINGS FOR THE LONG /e/ VOWEL SOUND

e	ee	ie	ea	e_e	y	ey

sleep

tree

very

feel

see

dizzy

rocky

deep

weeks

fluffy

keep

hungry

creep

happy

me

baby

seem

peep